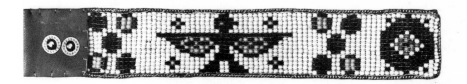

INDIAN BEAD STRINGING & WEAVING

By RUTH SCHOLZ-PETERS

STERLING PUBLISHING CO., INC.   NEW YORK

Oak Tree Press Co., Ltd. London & Sydney

OTHER BOOKS OF INTEREST

Beads Plus Macramé
Creating Silver Jewelry with Beads
Creating with Beads
Finger Weaving: Indian Braiding

Translated by Maxine Hobson

Copyright © 1975 by Sterling Publishing Co., Inc.
419 Park Avenue South, New York, N.Y. 10016
Distributed in Australia and New Zealand by Oak Tree Press Co., Ltd.,
P.O. Box J34, Brickfield Hill, Sydney 2000, N.S.W.
Distributed in the United Kingdom and elsewhere in the British Commonwealth
by Ward Lock Ltd., 116 Baker Street, London W 1
Originally published under the title "Perlen Gewebt und Gefädelt,"
© 1974 by Verlag Frech, Stuttgart-Botnang, Germany.
Manufactured in the United States of America
All rights reserved
Library of Congress Catalog Card No.: 75–14524
Sterling ISBN 0–8069–5334–9 Trade   Oak Tree 7061–2183–X
5335–7 Library

Contents

Illus. 1.

Beads—Woven and Strung

Decorative beads have a very long history. We know that the Venetians were importing beads from the glassworks of Egypt as much as 3,000 years ago. Thereafter, Bohemia—a kingdom not far from Venice—became the major supplier to the Western world. Beads at that time were either cylindrical or fused glass. Cylindrical beads were cut from long, slender glass tubes; fused glass beads were likewise cut from tubes, then shaken about in glowing-hot iron drums until their edges became round.

The greatest time for bead handwork came in the 19th century—examples of it that still exist are now sought-after antiques. Your great-grandmothers very likely practiced this beautiful handicraft, stringing beads, weaving them or incorporating them in their embroidery. Today, beads are back in fashion and stringing or weaving with beads has become a fascinating hobby.

The variety of types and sizes of beads available as well as the enormous range of colors now being produced add to the beauty of the beadwork itself. Traditional designs and motifs of the American Indians are especially attractive when carried out in beadwork.

The many projects in this book will give you suggestions for objects you can make yourself and, hopefully, inspire you to get started working with beads.

The Variety of Beads and How to Work with Them

Small glass beads, called seed beads, range from 1/16 to 3/16 inch (1 to 4 mm.) in diameter. The smaller size is especially good for embroidery and weaving Indian beadwork. Large seed beads are easier to use for stringing. Bigger beads are usually made of plastic and you can buy round, oval, flat, tubular or barrel-shaped beads. Porcelain tile and wooden beads are also available in many sizes.

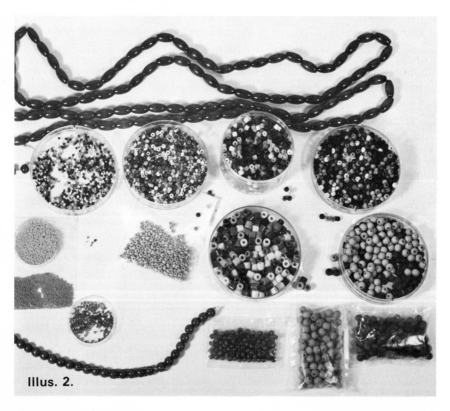

Illus. 2.

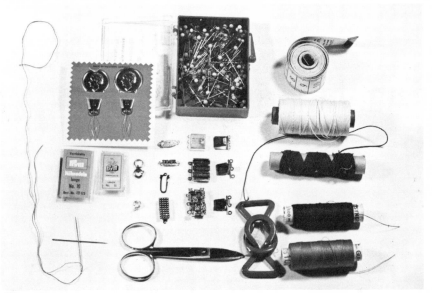

Illus. 3.

Traditional beads are opaque and the choice of colors is almost unlimited, including two-tone, striped and multi-colored varieties. Beads are sold in plastic vials, bags or boxes which are useful for keeping them sorted.

Use synthetic thread to string or weave small beads. Work large beads on specially made linen beading thread or thin nylon string. You can use either single or doubled strings, provided the hole in the beads is large enough. For stringing stretch bracelets, napkin rings, or similar items you must use an elastic thread. Beading needles are similar to sewing needles, but somewhat longer and not so sharply pointed. You will need a fine (thin) needle for working with the tiny seed beads.

Beads, needles, thread, as well as findings, such as clasps for arm and neckbands, belt buckles, and frames for coin purses and handbags, are available in hobby or craft supply shops.

Each item of beadwork is usually made with only one size bead, although there are likely to be slight differences of size within any assortment of beads. To make it easier to pick out the beads you want, separate them according to color in flat plastic bowls or lids before you start to string or weave.

Simple Stringing

Children often play with sets of large wooden beads, stringing them one after the other onto a long shoelace. You can use this same simple technique to make an attractive glass-bead necklace. For this you will need two bags of colored glass beads, a needle and a string about 6 feet (or 2 metres) long. String the beads on in groups—10 or 12 beads of the same color—using as many different colors as you have before repeating the sequence. Here you can also work with two different sizes of beads. This necklace is worn looped around the neck several times.

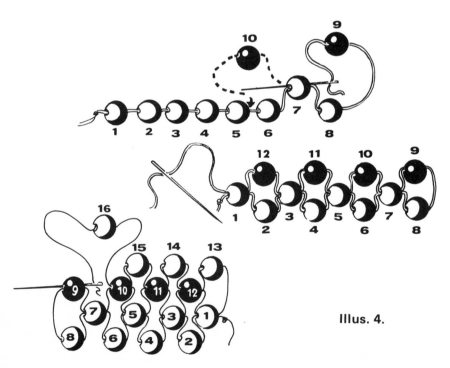

Illus. 4.

8

You can also use wooden beads in assorted colors to make three separate necklaces of various lengths to create the same effect. Use the same color beads and elastic thread to make five matching bracelets. Push the beginning and end knots inside a bead. This is all it takes to produce some pieces of really fashionable jewelry.

To start a piece of flat beadwork, you must string and then bind together several individual beads, using just a needle and string. Beginning a piece of flat beadwork is not so easy because at first you have only a few beads lying in your hand to hold onto. To learn the technique, make a trial piece or two. Once you have mastered this stringing, the work goes quickly.

Following the steps in the diagram, thread 8 medium-sized wooden beads of the same color on the string, knotting the thread at the end to hold the first bead securely in place. Leave some space between the other beads. Lay the strung beads on your left hand between your thumb and index finger with the knot away from you, the thread pointing towards you. For the

Illus. 5. The easiest way to work with beads is to simply thread them onto a long string. An assortment of bright colors creates an attractive effect.

next row, use beads of a different color to make the steps easier to follow in the sample piece. Put bead #9 on the string and then run the string back through bead #7. Put bead #10 on the string and go back through bead #5, following the same procedure for beads #11 and #3, #12 and #1. Now, turn the work in your hand so the thread once again points toward your body. Begin the next row by adding bead #13, then running the string back through bead #12. Finish the third row in the same manner, turning the work when you come to the end of the row.

With this stringing technique, you build up rows of beads one after the other. Each new row fills in the spaces left between the beads of the row before. You can see the bead pattern clearly as soon as the first few rows are worked. To run the string back through the already-threaded beads, turn them slightly so that the needle passes through at an angle to the work. In starting a piece of work, you must use an even number of beads. With this basic technique, you can easily carry out the projects on the following pages.

TABLE MATS

Porcelain tile beads are especially suited for making simple table mats. For a medium-size table mat, string 20 beads on a nylon thread or special tile cord. Porcelain tile beads usually have holes large enough to take several thicknesses of cord. Knot the first bead on the end of the string. Lay the strung beads in your left hand with the knot away from you, the thread with the needle pointing towards you. Pick up a new bead, #21, on the cord and pass the needle and cord back through bead #19. Add bead #22, pass the cord back through bead #17, etc., until the row is finished. Turn the work in your hand and work the third row in the same manner. You will add 10 new beads for each new row. Continue adding rows until the mat is square. Since the possible pattern and color

Illus. 6.

Illus. 7. All of the articles on these two pages were made by stringing.

Illus. 8.

combinations are almost innumerable, you can always come up with a new idea.

To make a mat with sawtooth edges, you must work from the middle to the outside. String the beads for the widest part at the beginning, working all the way to one edge first, then from the middle again out to the other edge. In each row, string 2 fewer beads than in the row before, and in this way, working out to the point. For a stepped-edge mat, decrease the number of beads per row according to a predetermined pattern. To make the stepped-edge mat in the illustration, start with a string of 38 beads. Add 19 beads each for rows 2–5, 18 beads for row 6, 17 beads for rows 7–11, 15 beads for row 12, 13 beads for rows 13–17, 12 beads for row 18, 11 beads for rows 19–23, 10 beads for row 24, 9 beads for rows 25–27, 7 beads for row 28, 5 beads for rows 29–33, 4 beads for row 34, and 3 beads for rows 35–38. Turn the work over and repeat the formula for the second half of the mat. (See page 48 for instruction on creating your own designs.)

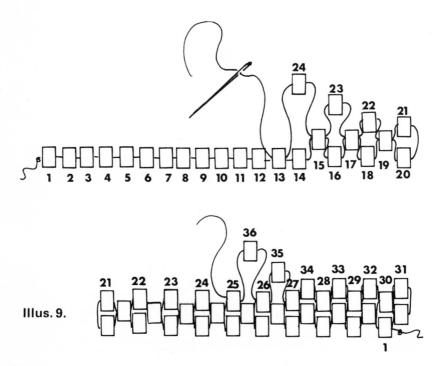

Illus. 9.

NECKBANDS AND HEADBANDS

Neckbands have an extraordinarily charming effect and they can be worked out in the most diverse patterns. The attractive, versatile bead material and the rich color spectrum of beads available will constantly encourage you to try new things. You can make wide or narrow neckbands using tiny seed beads or larger glass beads. You can also use small wooden beads if they are suitable to the kind of clothes you wear. It is an exciting challenge to choose the proper color beads to match or complement a particular outfit.

Start with a row of beads equal to the width of the band you want to make and go on adding rows until you reach the length you need. You will need to attach a suitable clasp, fastening one piece of it to each end of the work. Most of these clasps have a row of holes in them through which you pass your thread as you string the first and last rows of beads. You can adapt the designs from most of the objects shown in this book to decorative neckbands that you can easily string yourself.

Headbands worked out in striking patterns make distinctive jewelry for the hair. They are made like neckbands out of small glass or wooden beads. A convenient way to fasten them is to attach a narrow strip of self-adhering Velcro to each end of the beaded band. This also allows you to adjust the size to suit your hairstyle of the moment.

Illus. 10.

(left)
Illus. 11. This headband was woven on a loom, the neckband strung with a needle and thread. Weaving is best suited for patterns with vertical lines while stringing is best for patterns with diagonal lines.

(below)
Illus. 12. Follow this pattern and the directions on page 18 to make this unusual bracelet.

Illus. 13.

UNUSUAL COLORED ARM BANDS
AND BRACELETS

You can take advantage of left-over, large and small wooden beads to make intriguing arm bands. For this simple new stringing technique, you will use a thin darning needle and elastic thread.

The basic scheme for stringing the individual beads together is shown in Illus. 12. Put 2 large, then 3 small beads on the thread. Knot the first bead in the end of the string, then pass the needle back through the last large bead. Again string 2 large and 3 small beads, passing the thread back through the last large one. Continue working this way until the bracelet reaches the proper length. Knot the two ends of the thread together, put a drop of glue on the knot and push it into a bead.

By varying the size, numbers, and colors of the beads you can create many different results.

NECKTIES

A beaded tie is something really different. First, work a narrow or wide band about 12 inches (30 cm.) long in a selected design. Make a separate narrow ring, worked like a napkin ring (page 20), just the size to slide over one end of the band. This is the "knot." Secure it with a stitch so that it can't slide down. Work 2 narrow bands just 2 beads wide out from the top of the tie to serve to hold it around your neck. When these bands are the right length for your neck, attach a necklace clasp. (See in color on page 17.)

STRETCH BRACELETS

Bracelets made of strung beads are especially decorative. The effect is magnified when you wear a bracelet and neckband that match. The design possibilities are practically endless. You can use tiny beads for a delicate arrangement, but larger beads,

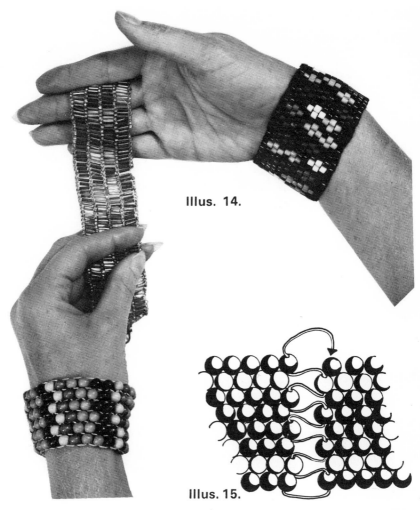

Illus. 14.

Illus. 15.

cylindrical beads, porcelain tile and wooden beads are also suitable.

The width of the clasp must be equal to the width of the beaded band. Here, also, one part is attached to each end of the band.

To make a simple slip-on band, string the beads on elastic cord. Close the band by fastening the ends together with the elastic thread. Run the thread back and forth, passing the needle through the beads on both ends, as shown in the diagram, until the band is closed. Knot the elastic at the end and push the knot into a bead.

NAPKIN RINGS

Napkin rings can be made of glass, wood, or porcelain tile beads. Since one of the purposes of a napkin ring is to keep napkins from being mixed up, be sure to use different color beads for each one, especially if you make them all of the same designs.

Work napkin rings on linen beading thread, nylon string or elastic cord. Whichever threading material you use, run it through the beads at the ends of the band to join them together into a completed ring. Handmade napkin rings make useful gifts.

Illus. 17.

COIN PURSES, EYEGLASS CASES
AND HANDBAGS

Bags made of beads are unusual and this factor alone gives them a certain charm. The metal frames for coin purses, eyeglass cases, and handbags are available in many different sizes and styles. For small bags, use large glass beads strung on doubled synthetic thread. For purses use small porcelain tile beads (small tile beads are bigger than large glass beads). Use linen beading thread for handbags.

Bags are worked directly on the frame, which comes with a series of holes already in it. The first step is to attach a row of beads to the frame running from corner to corner of the top edge of the frame. Put 2 beads on the string and knot the first bead securely at the end of the thread. With the frame opened up, run the string from back to front (from the inside out) through one of the corner holes. Moving towards the middle of the frame (towards the clasp in the picture) run the thread back in through the second hole. String 2 more beads and go through the next hole from back to front and then go inside again through the following hole. Continue in this manner until the top edge of the frame is lined with beads.

Now, using the basic stringing technique, add row after row of beads. Pass the thread through the holes in the sides of the frame as the rows reach the proper level. Always run the needle from inside out and back in through the next hole. Work this way down to the frame hinge, then do the same thing to the other half of the frame. As you pass the hinge, the two pieces of flat beadwork should be of the same length and you need to join them together at their edges. At the end of one of the beaded rows, where you left off at the hinge, put 4 to 6 beads on the thread and go under the hinge, passing the needle through the first bead in the bottom row on the other side. Run the string through the row right to the end, and again put 4–6 beads on the thread, passing under the hinge to the first bead in the bottom row on the other side. The work is a closed ring now and you can add beads in a continuous circle, using the basic stringing technique. When you reach the desired length, close

Illus. 18.

the frame and lay the work flat, one side on top of the other. To close up the bottom, run the thread through a bead on one side, then through a bead on the opposite side, working from one end to the other.

For further embellishment, you can add fringes or bead scallops to the bottom.

As the final step, sew a taffeta lining in the purse, a leather one in the large bags. Stitch the top of it to the row of beads attached to the frame.

NECKLACES WITH PENDANTS

Pendants are something very special. During the past several years they have really caught on as fashion jewelry. Pendants make amusing, stylish accessories for a wide variety of outfits.

In the available selection of material, glass beads in particular stand out. The large number of styles shown in this book demonstrate how diversely pendants can be fashioned. Medium-sized glass beads are the right size for most pendants.

To string a pendant, you always start with the widest part. You then use the stringing technique to work out in both

Illus. 19.

Illus. 20.

Illus. 21.

directions. Of course, you can leave blank sections or add strips of beads as you go. Because of the variation in the exact size and shape of bead material, your own project may turn out a slightly different shape than the examples shown here.

The type with rows of single beads passing through an open middle space is particularly charming. The pendant is worked in two pieces. String a narrow rectangular band for the upper piece, then a tapered one for the bottom, with hanging strings of beads at the end. Make the tapered piece by starting with the wide rows at the top and using progressively fewer beads as you add rows. When you come to the end of the narrowest row at the bottom, string more beads on the thread and wind the beaded string around the work several times to create the knot-like appearance. Use the same thread without breaking it to make the long fringes. Put 25 or so beads on the thread, turn the last bead to serve as a stop and run the thread back up through the rest of the beads. Then join the two pieces with 8 strands of beads.
(See Illus. 19.)

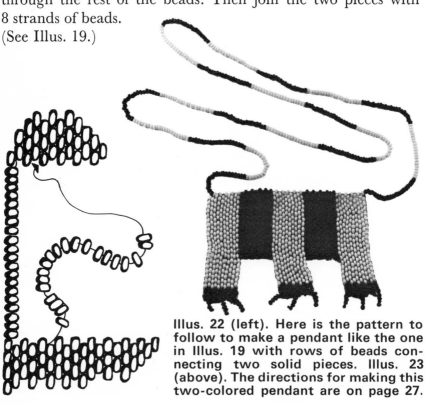

Illus. 22 (left). Here is the pattern to follow to make a pendant like the one in Illus. 19 with rows of beads connecting two solid pieces. Illus. 23 (above). The directions for making this two-colored pendant are on page 27.

To make the free-form pendant with the terraced effect at the bottom, begin stringing in the middle, the widest part. String 36 beads. Add 10 rows of 18 beads. For the next 8 rows, leave off 2 beads at the beginning and end of each row for the "step." Now string 10 more rows, leaving off 3 beads at the beginning and end of each row, again for the step. For the bottom step, do 9 rows of only 4 beads.

Work now in the opposite direction, stringing two beaded bands upwards from the wide middle piece. String 20 rows of 6 beads at each side. Add short curved strings of beads at the ends of these strips to finish up the top of the pendant. Fasten the necklace strings to the top and, finally, add the fringes at the corners of the steps. (See Illus. 20.)

In stringing the diagonal-stripe pendant, you must begin at the upper corner. Start with 32 beads on the thread. Add rows of 16 beads until you complete a piece that is almost square.

For the extensions to the pendant, continue using the same thread to work 15 rows of 6 beads. At the bottom, trim with bead fringes, still using the same thread. As before, string the beads for a fringe and then run the thread back through all the beads except the bottom one. Now run through the next two beads in the bottom row of the pendant and make another fringe. String all the fringes in the same way.

Make the second extension also by adding 15 rows of 6 beads, but this time you will have to start a new thread. (See Illus. 21.)

Work the two-colored pendant exactly the same as the previous ones. Here, too, the three lower parts are joined to the main piece by stringing them right into the bottom row of beads. To make the necklace strings, run a doubled thread through the top row of beads and string enough beads on the thread to reach the desired length. Run the end of the thread into the pendant and back across the work before fastening it. (See Illus. 23.)

BELTS

Belts made of beads really attract attention. Worn with a dress or a sweater, they provide a touch of individuality. Here,

Illus. 24.

Illus. 25.

also, the color of the beads can be chosen to harmonize with a particular item of clothing or to set off a special outfit. Use larger beads to string belts and choose sturdy cotton or nylon cord to make the belt durable. Belts made of porcelain tile beads are effective because the beads lie next to each other very evenly. A belt made of wooden beads is more suitable for a rustic dress. The beaded band for a belt must be strung to the exact length required, since the position of the clasp usually is not adjustable. You can also use the type of fastener found on bikini tops or bras to fasten belts. Attach one part of whatever closure you use to each end of the beaded band, threading it right in with the beads if possible.

Illus. 26.

EARRINGS

Use small, left-over glass beads to make earrings to harmonize with neckbands, belts or pendants.

You will need a pair of perforated discs attached to clips to serve as the base for your beads. Hobby shops and craft dealers can supply them inexpensively. Sew beads on the disc and then attach it to the clip with the fastener. Add strings of beads or fringes to the bottom of the disc as trimming.

Small strings of beads can just as easily be attached directly to a pair of clips. String large glass or small porcelain tile beads on a thin piece of silver wire and close it into a ring. Fasten the ring to the clip with a silver loop.

Illus. 27.

RINGS

To make bead rings, use finger-ring findings which have the same kind of perforated disc as the earring findings. Sew beads to the mesh. You can use various sizes of beads in the design. Run the needle and thread up through the middle hole of the disc and pick up a bead. Now run the thread down through the next hole and then back up again with the thread. Once more pick up a bead. Continue working this way from the middle to the outside until the entire disc is covered with beads.

Lay the completed disc on the ring and bend the fasteners carefully to lock the two pieces together.

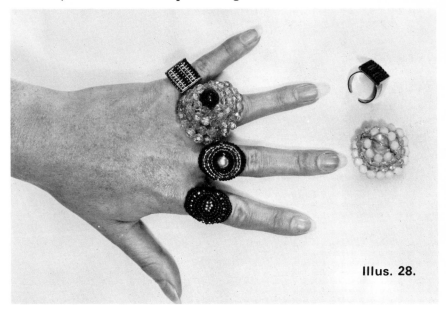

Illus. 28.

Weaving with Beads

Stringing beads is a craft that has been known for generations. Weaving with them is less well known, although the work produced with this technique is uniform, symmetrical, and compact. Weaving allows you to carry out precise patterns. Since weaving results in work with straight vertical and horizontal rows of beads compared to the horizontal and diagonal lines of strung work, it makes different kinds of designs possible —especially lettering.

Illus. 29.

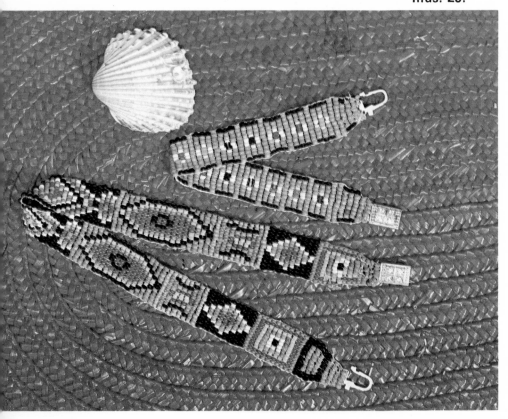

In every piece of weaving, you work across threads stretched the length of a weaving frame. Ready-made frames are available in various widths and sizes, but for your first project you can make a weaving frame from the Styrofoam lid of a shipping carton or something similar. Stick a row of glass-topped pins in each of the narrow ends of the lid to hold the stretched threads.

Illus. 30.

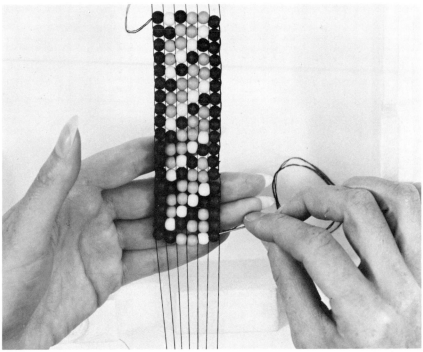

STYROFOAM WEAVING FRAME

For your first trial piece, put 7 pins in each side to stretch 7 strings. Knot the thread around the first pin at one end, pull it down to the opposite end and pass it around the first and second pins. Run it back to the opposite end and around the second and third pins. Continue this until you reach the last pin where you end and tie the thread. Use a needle and thread to do the actual weaving. Holding one of the ends with pins closest to you, tie the end of the thread to the left string at a point about 8 inches (20 cm.) up from the end of the box. Pick up 6 beads on the thread and push them down to the knot. Now run the beaded thread under the stretched strings from left to right. With your left fingers, press the beaded thread tightly up against the stretched strings, with one bead between each of them. Run the needle back through the beads, making sure the string passes over the top of the stretched threads. This locks the beads securely to the threads. When the first row is

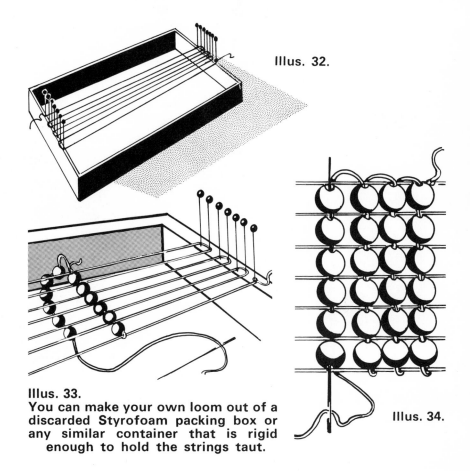

Illus. 33.
You can make your own loom out of a
discarded Styrofoam packing box or
any similar container that is rigid
enough to hold the strings taut.

Illus. 34.

finished, pick up 6 more beads and work another row the
same way. Continue working row after row, pushing the completed rows tightly together as you go.

When the work is completed, weave the ends of the stretched
strings (called the "warp") into the piece and tie them. Undo one
string at a time, working from the outside towards the middle.
Leave the work attached to the frame until, of course, you come
to the last thread.

Before beginning any weaving project, you must measure out
the length of the warp strings exactly. If you are making a
14-inch (35-cm.) neckband, for example, you should leave
about 8 inches (20 cm.) of thread at each end for weaving back
into the work or to fasten to a clasp. This means you will need a
box about 30 inches (75 cm.) long.

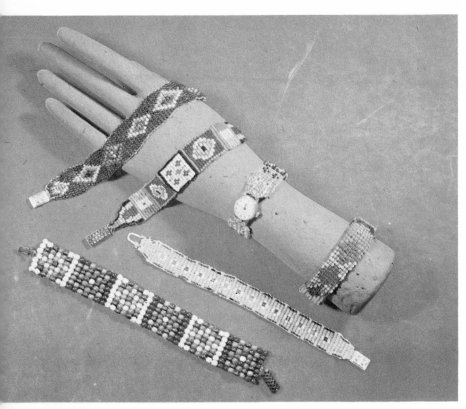

Illus. 35.

ATTACHING THE WARP STRINGS TO A CLASP

For arm and neckbands you can avoid sewing in the warp strings by fastening them directly to a clasp. The exact length of the finished work must be calculated before you start. Both ends of the clasp are secured with string and pins to the edges of the lid so that the eyes on the clasp face inwards. Use a needle to pull a long thread from one part of the clasp to the other, passing the thread through the appropriate holes. If your project calls for more threads across than there are holes in the clasp, then you will have to run more than one thread through some of the holes. Since the length of the work is fixed, you can, if you want, weave from the middle down to the clasp on one

Illus. 36.

side, then turn the loom around and work from the middle down to the other end of the clasp.

When you come near the end of your weaving thread, run it back through a few beads and tie it. Do the same to start a new thread.

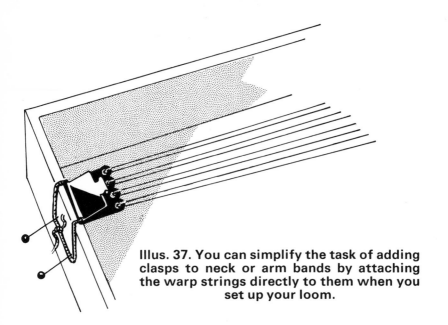

Illus. 37. You can simplify the task of adding clasps to neck or arm bands by attaching the warp strings directly to them when you set up your loom.

Illus. 38. All sorts of scrap material are suitable for making bead-weaving looms.

COMMERCIALLY MADE WEAVING FRAMES

The weaving frame or loom shown here is made of metal. Cut the warp strings to the proper length and knot them together at one end. Fasten the knot to the knob on one of the roller spools. Turn the roller to wrap the threads around it one time. Bring the threads over the top of both metal thread guides to the opposite spool. Knot the threads together again and fasten the knot to the knob on the spool. Turn the spool, rolling up the threads until they are stretched tightly over the top of the loom. The advantage of this type loom is that you can make bands of beadwork much longer than the frame itself. Just wind the partially finished work around the first roller, drawing additional threads into place onto the loom from the second roller. This apparatus is particularly suited for delicate weaving with small seed beads.

BEADED HATBAND

A project that is often overlooked but very attractive, is a hatband made of beads. It can be woven of large glass, porcelain tile, or wooden beads. The band is made to the diameter of the hat. Tie the warp strings from both sides together where they meet. If you want just a narrow beaded band to go in the middle of the regular hatband, you must sew it tightly in place on the hat with some invisible stitches.

You can create quite an effect by weaving several bands in various colors or types of beads and interchanging them to match the color of your hatband to your dress every time.

WOVEN NECKBANDS

It was a popular style in your great-grandmother's day to wear delicately woven neckbands. For the most part, they were made in dark shades; the fashion was to maintain a "serious" look. Today, however, we love color.

Tiny seed beads are ideal for weaving neckbands. The smaller the beads, the more distinctly the pattern will stand out. Use as few as 6 beads in a row for narrow bands, as many as 14 beads in a row for wider bands. When you are working with larger glass, wood or porcelain tile beads, you should use between 4 and 8 beads to a row. Attach clasps to the ends to hold the neckbands in place. Work the somewhat longer headbands in the same manner, but to fasten them, sew two strips of Velcro onto the ends of the band.

The possible variations in subject, ornamentation and pattern are innumerable. One of the special charms of weaving your own neckbands, though, is in being able to choose a color or design to match or complement a specific article of clothing.

Illus. 41.

Illus. 42.

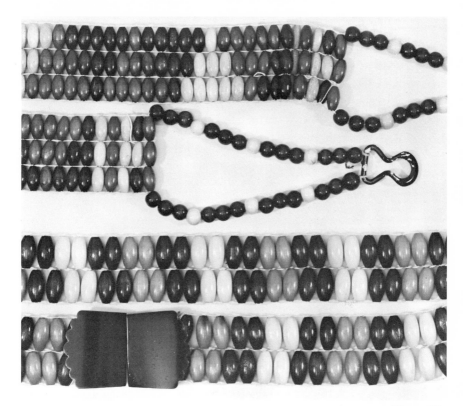

DECORATED BELTS

Weaving with large wood or porcelain tile beads produces work with a very even appearance due to the symmetry of the beads themselves. Large oval beads are especially ornamental. Just 2 or 3 of them to a row provide the width you need for most belts, allowing the handwork to go quickly. For weaving belts with large beads, you will need a Styrofoam lid that is at least half as long as the finished piece will be. Run the warp threads all the way around the lid, front, back, and sides, keeping them at uniform intervals from each other. Fasten the ends together at the back. Weave the strings on the front of the lid with beads first, and when you need more strings, just slide the work around the lid until you again have empty strings stretched across the top. Continue working this way until you reach the proper length including the buckle width. Cut the left-over warp strings in the middle and fasten them to the buckle.

If you want to avoid moving the work, make a band as long as the front of the lid allows, then lengthen the piece with beaded strings and fasten the ends of the clasp to them. To work with wide beads on a metal frame loom, just leave two or more thread dividers between warp strings.

Illus. 44.

44

PENDANTS

Almost no other jewelry item shows beadwork off to such advantage as a decorative pendant. A well-made and designed pendant gives a special touch to the wearer.

The effect of a pendant can be graceful or rustic, according to the shape and the type of bead you choose. Through the design you can express your own ideas, and through your own individual handwork you can make something very personal. Each piece comes out differently according to your choice of beads. You must build up a hanging ornament symmetrically, but you can make it long and stretched-out or short and wide. Add fringes or beaded circles to both sides of the flat basic shape, extending the form. Follow the diagrams for instructions on how to finish up a pendant with fringes or looped, beaded strings as extra decoration. The remaining warp strings must be carefully run back through the work above and below, then sewn in.

Any bead material can be used for pendants. Seed beads, larger glass beads, porcelain tile, or small wooden beads are worked exactly the same way. When you weave with the smallest mini-beads you obtain almost the effect of petit-point needlework, except that through the character of the beads, the pendant takes on a special luminosity.

Attach the pendant to a simple string of beads.

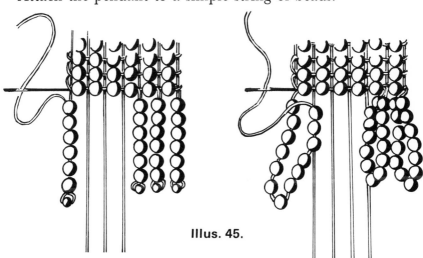

Illus. 45.

JEWELRY FOR THE WRIST

Distinctive, extraordinary designs can be worked out in woven arm bands. You can weave narrow, wide, single color, or multi-colored bands with decorations exactly to the wishes of the wearer. Make arm bands for evening wear with gold or silver beads. It is quite stylish to wear several arm bands on your wrist at the same time as you do with other jewelry. If you have the patience, you can even make a matching set of ornaments—arm band, neckband, earrings, and pendant.

Illus. 46

Illus. 47.

EXAMPLES FOR CREATING YOUR OWN DESIGNS

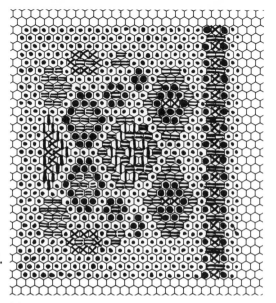

Illus. 48.

To plan your own motif, ornament, or pattern, draw it out on honeycomb graph paper for stringing, on regular square graph paper for weaving. Use crayons or colored pencils to test out various color combinations.

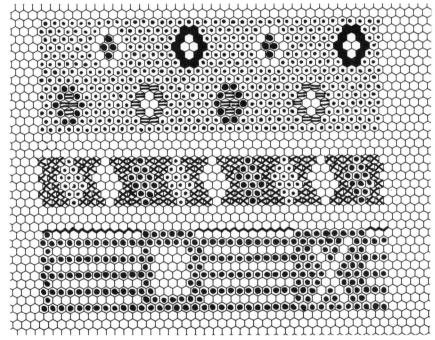

Illus. 49.

Illus. 50.

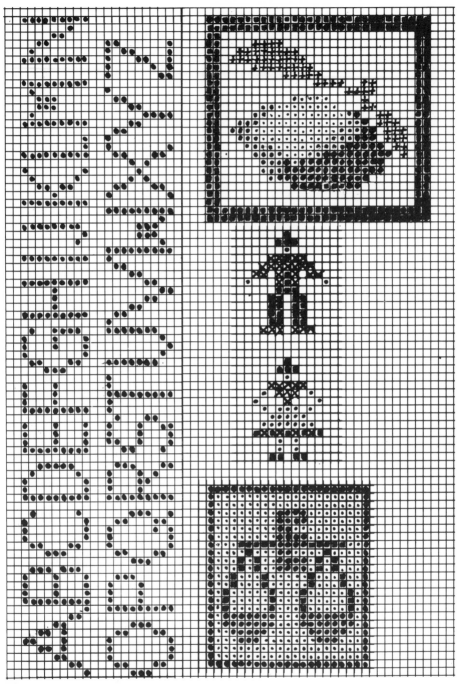

Illus. 51.

Illus. 52.

A Gallery of American Indian Beadwork

Illus. 53. This dance collar is the work of the Tlingit Indians of southern Alaska. Much Indian work consists of lengths of beads threaded on strings which were laid in position according to the pattern and then sewn in place. The rows of beads were secured by an overlay stitch between every two or three beads. These designs can be adapted readily as patterns for stringing or weaving.

Illus. 54. OGLALA SIOUX, deerskin decorated with beads in a geometric pattern.

Illus. 55. YANKTON SIOUX, woman's buckskin dress.

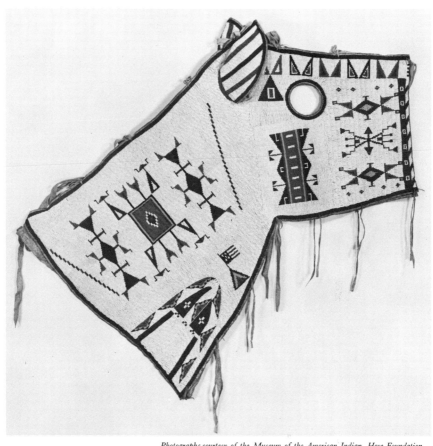

Illus. 56. TETON SIOUX, horse head cover.

Illus. 57. COMANCHE, baby carrier.

Illus. 58. ESKIMO, beaded pipe bag.

Illus. 59.

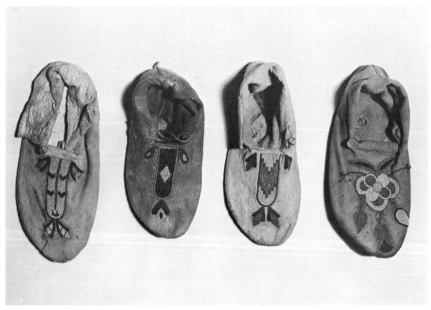

Illus. 60.
CROW, beaded moccasins.

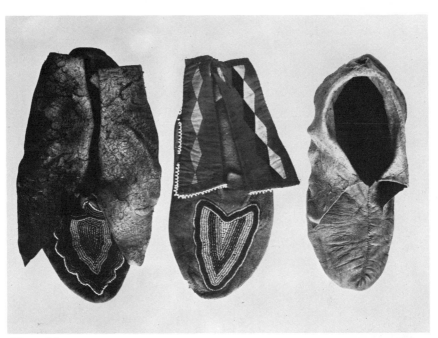

Illus. 61.

Illus. 62.
SHAWNEE, beaded moccasins.

Illus. 63. SHAWNEE, beaded shoulder bag.

Illus. 64. CHIPPEWA, cloth bag.

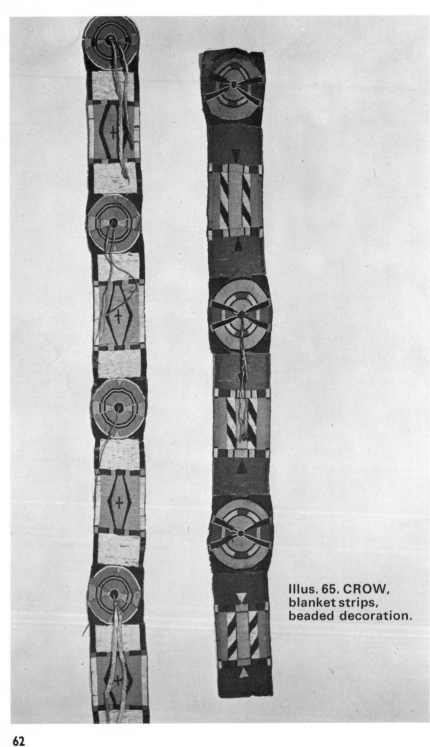

Illus. 65. CROW,
blanket strips,
beaded decoration.

Illus. 66. NORTHERN CHEYENNE, beaded buckskin baby cap.

Photographs courtesy of the Museum of the American Indian, Heye Foundation

Illus. 67. OGLALA SIOUX, leather bag, beaded decoration.

Index